THE ARTS OF INDIA

Ajit Mookerjee

THE ARTS OF INDIA

FROM PREHISTORIC
TO MODERN TIMES

Revised & Enlarged

CHARLES E. TUTTLE CO.: PUBLISHERS
Rutland, Vermont & Tokyo, Japan

to Sudha

REPRESENTATIVES
FOR CONTINENTAL EUROPE:
BOXERBOOKS, INC., ZURICH

FOR THE BRITISH ISLES:
PRENTICE-HALL INTERNATIONAL, INC., LONDON

FOR AUSTRALASIA:
PAUL FLESCH & CO., PTY. LTD., MELBOURNE

PUBLISHED BY CHARLES E. TUTTLE COMPANY, INC.
OF RUTLAND, VERMONT & TOKYO, JAPAN
WITH EDITORIAL OFFICES
AT SUIDO 1-CHOME, 2–6, BUNKYO-KU, TOKYO

LIBRARY OF CONGRESS CATALOG
CARD NO. 66–17557

FIRST PRINTING, 1966

BOOK DESIGN, TYPOGRAPHY & LAYOUT BY KEN TREMAYNE

PRINTED IN JAPAN

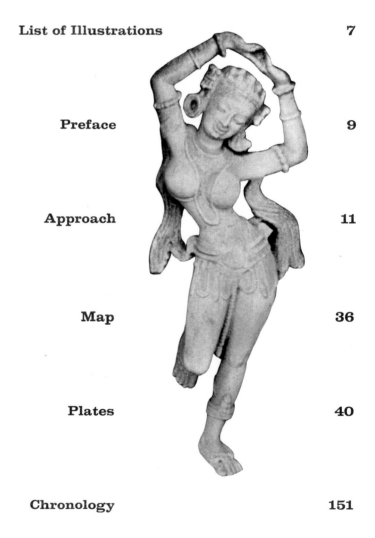

A. *Nayika figure from Bhubanesvara,* c. *100 A.D. (reproduced on jacket in color).*

The Arts of India: LIST OF ILLUSTRATIONS

THE SPIRITUAL AND MATERIAL ASPECTS OF INDIAN LIFE ARE as significant as those of any other country—India too manifests its sacrifice and understanding, achievement and frustration, toil and greed.

The sages of India found solace in meditation and tried to unfold the mysteries of the universe manifest in matter and energy, atoms and stars, and the people sweated and struggled for all that the world could give. They established kingdoms and empires, administered vast territories, produced generals and statesmen, artists and poets, musicians and mathematicians, philosophers and astronomers. Their ships sailed across the oceans, and, in turn, from all over the world came traders in search of secret treasures.

Colonists from India moved to distant lands and established flourishing communities beyond the seas; their cultural missions crossed over snow-clad mountain peaks; their architects and artists made temples, statues and paintings of enduring strength and beauty.

A pilgrim journeying along the road of eternity will meet the monuments raising their spires and again falling into pieces, leaving only fragments to remind us of the departed glory. But the tradition remains unbroken. It is the great folk tradition that will continue to inspire our future generations for ages to come.

My thanks are due to the Government of India, The Archaeology Survey and the National Museum, New Delhi; Calcutta University and Prof. D.P. Ghosh, Curator, Asutosh Museum; Bharat Kala Bhawan, Banaras; Census of India, for permission to use copyright material. I have taken the greatest care to trace the owners of the photographs or other materials incorporated but should like to be forgiven in case any name has been inadvertently omitted in this connection.

I am also grateful to Mr. Samar Sen, Dr. Kalyan K. Ganguli, Mr. Amiya Jiban Mookerjee, Mr. Sudhansu Chowdhury and Mr. G. M. Primlani for their valuable cooperation and particularly to Mr. Ken Tremayne for assistance in bringing out the second edition.

A.M.

The Arts of India: APPROACH

BEYOND THE HIGHLY CIVILIZED CITIES OF HARAPPA AND Mohenjo-daro in the Indus valley, which flourished some five thousand years ago, traces of palaeolithic and neolithic culture have been found in many parts of India. The rock shelters of central and northern India are now known to be repositories of the earliest manifestation of pictorial art in this subcontinent. Standing out dimly upon the rough walls of these caves are seen drawings of animals and men generally representing hunting scenes and other group activities. Numerous rock paintings discovered at such places as Singanpur, Mirzapur, Hoshangabad, are strongly akin to the prehistoric cave paintings of Spain.

The hunting scene in Singanpur cave, where a group of hunters is struggling to capture a bison, is a forceful presentation in mauve, pale yellow and burgundy. A similar scene in Mirzapur cave depicts the death agony of a wounded boar. Although many of these rock paintings are now undecipherable, and some having been covered by later drawings, enough is preserved to testify to the dynamic vision of the prehistoric artist.

Our knowledge, however, of this earliest art form, with all the fascination it offers, remains embryonic. But the art of the Indus valley is at once more familiar and comprehensive. The clear and coherent conceptions of plastic art which confront us for the first time at Harappa and Mohenjo-daro are undoubtedly the culmination of artistic traditions of centuries.

This was the turning point and with it Indian sculpture in the proper sense began. And it began with such a rich promise that René Grousset, while studying a Mohenjo-daro earthenware statuette of a seated monkey, remarks that "it may well foreshadow the whole art of Indian animal sculpture, from capitals of Asoka to the *ratha* of Mavalipuram.'' It is not in animal forms alone that the art of Indus valley anticipates the subsequent development of Indian sculpture. Among the many small fragments of sculpture so far discovered in these sites are figures of a dancer and a dancing girl and a small torso of plastic subtlety. These statuettes bear witness to the ease and certitude with which the artist of the Indus valley handled the various plastic mediums like terracotta, ivory, bronze and alabaster.

Unlike their contemporaries in Egypt or Babylon, the Mohenjo-daro artists did not go in for the spectacular. They did not evolve a monumental art. No temples or palaces which point to a dominant kingship or priesthood have been found in the cities that have been explored. Perhaps social life and religious expression in the Indus valley civilization did not demand such art forms. But there are public baths, granaries, well-constructed houses, wide thoroughfares, and an intricate system of drainage which speak of an expansive and dignified civic life.

Art in the Indus valley, therefore, was conceived on a scale in which it could belong to the life of the people. The host of terracotta figurines, symbolic of a matriarchal culture, with their freshness of primeval joy, are representative of a folk tradition and link Mohenjo-daro with the prehistoric world. Most of the female figures center around fertility. But in the absence of attributes, one does not know whether they stand for goddesses or human beings.

The mother and child group expresses a subconscious notion of the potential powers of woman. There is a total disregard for accuracy in anatomical details, but in each case the figurine is full of life, possessing a natural, quiet dis-

B. *Indus Valley Seal*

tinction, and a pride of fulfilment. The enigmatic expression of the mother gives her a feeling of a mysterious withdrawal; the rather compressed mouth and strong, queer, arched brows reveal an immobility which is the primeval root of all beauty. Another innate virtue of the primitive mind, sensitiveness to color, expresses itself in endless varieties of illuminated potteries so abundantly found in Harappa and other Indus valley sites.

Of particular interest are the engravings on the seals that have been found in large numbers in Mohenjo-daro. The pictographic script which appears on some may eventually provide a clue to their use, but has not yet been deciphered. The subject of the engravings is usually an animal, the types most frequently represented being the humped or Brahmani bulls and unicorns. In the exquisite modeling of the bulls, the majesty and restrained vigor of the beast are strikingly conveyed. They are so successfully animated as to impart life into the figures which have otherwise a sphinx-like serenity.

Further, though sculpture of the human figure in the round has rarely survived, what has survived bears witness to the sense of volume characteristic of mature sculpture. This is illustrated at its best in the limestone statuette of a nude dancing figure from Harappa. The warm and lively body of a young male, revealing himself in contour, had never probably come so true in the medium of stone. Another illustration of this type can be found in a bronze statuette of a nude dancing girl from Mohenjo-daro. The sensitive molding of her back, the tense poise of her legs, are most significant. "But above all," says Iqbal Singh, "in the subtle comprehension of the dynamic expression which forms, as it were, an invisible background to her whole frame, plastic representation achieves a quality of perfection hardly surpassed even by the medieval South Indian bronzes."

The period is further marked by the emergence of phallic emblems, which indicated a growing male awareness that the source of generative power is the father, until then so long regarded as just a "way-opener." The discovery that male semen impregnates the female provided an important basis for the rise of the phallic cult, not only in India but most probably throughout the world. Even an anthropomorphic representation appears to be embodied in the figures of Pasupatinatha seated in a yogi pose, found at Mohenjo-daro, which is probably a direct predecessor of the later popular and powerful deity Siva, whose cult is closely associated with that of the lingam phallic symbol.

The Indus civilization did not collapse, as we commonly think, sometime about 2000 B.C., but was assimilated in successive stages of Indian life and thought. Although aesthetic history during the following fifteen centuries remains shrouded in mystery, and our lack of knowledge about any archaeological store of this period is unfortunate, we can be sure that the people who dwelt in India during those centuries were certainly no idlers.

Vedic burial mounds at Lauriya-Nandangarh and other places, which may be placed around 800 B.C. or thereabout, have yielded, among various objects, a small gold plaque bearing the figure of a nude female, probably the earth goddess mentioned in the burial hymns. A few more terracotta figurines of similar antiquity have also been found at Taxila, Bhita and other sites. The technique of execution is the same as in the Indus valley and the figurines have a close affinity which suggests a continuity in art traditions. Though very

few in number, they are of vital significance insofar as they provide the only link between the products of protohistoric age and the subsequent periods.

Literary evidence shows that the Vedic people were also experimenting with symbolic expressions that bore the transcendental excellence of their thought and emotion. Their attainment in meditative philosophy stands out even today as the finest ever achieved by man. For instance, the *Rig Veda,* the oldest Hindu scripture compiled as early as 1500 B.C., reveals a knowledge of the awakening of the human soul and its eternal inquiries into the mysteries of the universe.

This has been intensified in the *Upanishads,* which in a masterly way analyze the divinity and the destiny of the soul, its evolution through a process of searching towards the ultimate reality, and the merging into it of life and death, of energy and substance.

In the world of contemplation the Vedic people were soaring high, and their experiments in art expression became as universal as their profound questions. In this approach, "The cry of 'Not this! Not that!' which echoes so frequently in the *Up nishads,* is a confession not of ignorance, but of the breakdown of human language before the memory of that experience." Art became symbolic with vertical and horizontal lines, dots and circles conceived almost in spiritual dimension.

Throughout these periods, the fertility figurines following the Mohenjo-daro tradition continued to furnish the dominant motif. But the representation gradually tended to become archaic and stiff. It is only with the growth of Buddhism into a great popular religious movement that a comprehensive tradition of visual art emerged.

We must look upon the Buddhist art pattern as a whole. An extraordinary variety of contradictory and conflicting elements enter into the texture of this pattern. There are, to begin with, Asoka's capital on the one hand and reliefs of Bharhut and Sanchi on the other. These sculptures show the impress of two divergent techniques. The reliefs of Bharhut and Sanchi were derived from the indigenous tradition of wood and ivory carving, whereas the other was a comparatively stylized continuation from the early realism and as such an "aftermath of the Indus valley."

The Mauryan Empire flourished under Asoka during the third century B.C. Asoka's propagation of the Rule of Law followed his adoption of Buddhism as a state religion. Edicts of his imperial policy were conveyed through monolithic stone pillars, well-preserved specimens of which have come down to us. These columns of highly polished white sandstone are designed to stand by themselves without any architectural relation to their environment. The sheer columns rising up to forty feet are surmounted by capitals crowned with animated figures, lions being the most frequent. The well-known lion capital of Sarnath, one of the finest specimens, portrays the animal with striking realism and dignity. In spite of their artistic significance, the popular appeal of these capitals was limited owing to the didactic nature of their application.

On the other hand, a few large sculptures in the round from a folk tradition that survived can be placed in or before the Mauryan period. The material employed in all these examples is grey sandstone of a type similar to that used for the Asokan capitals. Equally significant is a small fragment of the same period portraying a weeping woman. The attitude of the

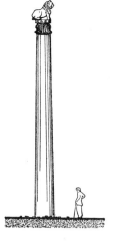

D. *Memorial column with lion capital*

figure, while singling out her individuality and dignity, makes her a universal symbol of sorrow rather than an episode from history. Though conceived in a limited space, the figure in relief somehow reproduces the massive grandeur which characterizes her contemporaries. The colossal standing female figure from Besnagar as well as a male torso from Baroda near Parkham have obviously the same tradition as the "Chauri-bearer," more properly known as Didarganj Yakshi. A *yakshi* is a female dryad, or tree spirit. In conception as well as execution, this figure is characterized by massive roundness which is almost "brutal in its affirmation" of a physical energy "not yet spiritualized." The specific purpose for which she was carved still remains a mystery—she stands however as a symbol of unity between the regal and eternal. She is an object of folklore, making life stir until one's blood runs warmer and quicker.

The warmth bursts into life immediately after Asoka, during the second century B.C., in the sculptured gateway and railings of the Buddhist stupa at Bharhut. The art of Bharhut is a popular art, an art appealing to and drawing its inspiration from the people. It seeks to help the common man find his position in the system of life in terms of values of his own existence. The scenes of the stone railings, medallions and gateways, therefore, derive their motifs from the woods, fields, and streams that surrounded the village folk—from the tales of the Buddha's birth, called Jatakas. Instead of the majestic lions of the Asokan capitals, there are familiar animals of the Indian scene. In the carvings of the *yakshis, yakshas* (the male counterpart of the former), and the *nagas,* the fertility deities of the village and the spirits of the woods and streams, in whom the simple people believed, the guild artists of

Bharhut were anticipating a psychological reality that was to receive its justification only in our own age.

A century later comes the stupa of Sanchi, with its magnificent gateways, even richer in ornament and invention than Bharhut. Although it follows the tradition of Bharhut, the Sanchi carvings show a definite sculptural advance. The figures are brought out in deeper light and shade. The primitive quality of Bharhut is gradually abandoned to impart a new spirit to the movement. The diversity of Jatakas is restricted, and though the friendly spirits of woods and streams reappear, they lose their familiar identity. The rendering on the whole attains an epic character away from introspection and simplicity.

Roughly contemporaneous with Sanchi are the rock-out *chaitya* caves of Western India—the best known examples of these shrines being those at Bhaja, Nasik, and Karli. Hewn out of living rock, these caves are apparently efforts to impart for the first time a stability to the architectural pattern hitherto practiced in wood and other perishable materials.

The sculpture panels associated with these chaitya halls derived inspiration from sources which had been responsible for the creation of the railing sculpture at Bodhgaya, a sculpture of massive corporeality, commemorating the place where the enlightened Buddha walked.

The craftsman of Mathura produced, from local material, graceful but highly sensuous figures during the first three centuries A.D. Here, the adaptation or transformation of sculpture to domestic needs came indeed as a silent revolution, and this sculpture had equally strong, religious, and domestic bearings. Most of the Mathura figures are not only three dimensional, but have dynamic characteristics that make

E. *Buddha image from Mathura*

the spectators move round them for a complete grasp. The technique as employed here has, again, a strong influence of indigenous claymodeling, giving the impression of "clay transmuted into stone."

The important feature of the Mathura "school" was the creation of an iconography which evolved through the actual portrayal of the Buddha and his saints, the Bodhisttavas, as well as of the saints of Jainism, the Tirthamakaras. At Bharhut, Sanchi, and elsewhere, it should be noted, the Buddha was never actually visually portrayed—only through symbols was the holy presence indicated.

The solidity and massiveness represented in the Mathura Buddha images are in interesting contrast with the numerous happy female figures—in company of birds, flowers, trees and flowing streams, mostly carved on railing pillars—"who stand," in the words of an ancient Indian writer, "in delicate poses and sportive attitudes with nimble waists and firm breasts, stealing the hearts of gods and men as it were with their teasing glances."

These *yakshis*—the glamor girls of Mathura—are typical examples of grace, charm and energy of youth revealed in stone.

While we find the Mathura style, notably in ivory carvings, spread beyond the boundaries of India, especially to Begram in Afganistan and as far as Pompeii in Italy, the north-western border province, known as Gandhara, with its capital at Taxila, had already a hybrid art which was "more interesting than beautiful."

Gandhara sculptures, with their varying qualities, were in the service of Buddhism, but in the absence of any date in

F. *A Gandhara Buddha*

the thousands of images discovered so far, it has been hard to determine their correct chronological sequence; nor does their style give any clue in that direction.

Tachose schist, a grey slate, was usually the material used for the carving of images. Huge Buddha statues, the largest being over 175 ft. in height, have been carved in stone in the rocks of Bamiyan in Afghanistan, a place dotted with Buddhist caves and monasteries. In the composition of these figures, lime was used where stone was not available, and castings of the faces in molds and plastering of bodies by the "stick-and-rag" technique were adopted. Innumerable images in the Hadda area serve as example.

There is a controversy over the place of Gandharan Buddha images in regard to the introduction of this device into the iconography of both Buddhism and Jainism: Were the Gandhara and the Mathura types produced simultaneously but independently? Coomaraswamy answers in the affirmative, and holds that they were done "in the middle or near the beginning of the first century A.D., and that only after the local types had been established did each effect the other."

Gandhara art however remains stereotyped and commonplace in the world of Indian art.

The duality of formal expression that we find in sculptures since the days of Asoka is apparent in later Buddhist art as well. The spiritual upsurge is trying to find expression through symbols, but at the same time, it is the triumph of life in all its material manifestation that is expressed through the lovingly molded contours of the dryads of Sanchi or the maidens of Mathura. And in later periods there are in frescoes on the walls of Ajanta caves, "that pictorial panorama with its endless

G. *Gate and railings from Barhut*

lyrical dreams and phantasies of the mystery of the female flesh and its promise of bliss."

The climax of the dual aspect may be witnessed at Amaravati, where in the second century A.D., "the most voluptuous and delicate flower of Indian sculpture" was produced. The main interest, however, is concentrated on the medallions and panelled friezes which have as their themes the Jataka stories of the birth and life of the Buddha. A design more complex in composition than anything produced previously distinguishes them and the supple carvings throb with a new linear rhythm destined to be developed more fully later. Two lines of carved stone slabs, 160 and 162 feet respectively in diameter, formed something like a wainscot round the stupas and the area of carving on the railing was 1700 sq. ft. Done mainly in the bas-relief tradition of Bharhut and Bodhgaya, they also incorporate some of the new features already noted in the sculptures at Mathura and Gandhara, namely that of depicting the Buddha in anthropomorphic form.

The Gupta period that followed saw the culmination of the creative efforts made hitherto and of the reorganization of all earlier experiments and experiences. For the first time, the political, social, cultural, and economic life of the country crystallized into a definite pattern and art also synchronized with this process. The formulas of aesthetic taste were established, passed on and later recorded in the manuals known as *shastras*. But instead of geometrical measurements, Gupta sculptures were expressed in curves found in the rhythms of nature. No realistic delineation of anatomy was allowed, joints and bones were hidden, and eternal youth had to be expressed through softly rounded limbs and placidly smooth faces. Art became sophisticatedly naive in this "golden age."

During this period the Buddha image was fully evolved. Its essential purpose was to satisfy a spiritual urge. The benign and compassionate face, the exquisitely beautiful gestures, or *mudras,* of hands—giving, blessing, reassuring, teaching, renouncing—all conveyed the spiritual message to the afflicted world. The sculptures tended towards abstraction—flesh becoming spirit, human form passing into divinity.

This was in fact an echo of the conception of the *Upanishads,* where man was regarded "not as a creature of the natural world, but as the vehicle of expression of an immortal and changeless spirit, the *atman.*" Very likely this abstraction was directly responsible for the creation of the multi-armed and multi-headed images in India, and those artists known as the *silpi-yogins,* in order to bring out the picture of the fuller reality that underlies the bodily form and movement, had to subject themselves to a strict spiritual discipline. This humility showed the desire of the artist to be in communion with the universal spirit. The classical quality of the *Dhyani* (mythical) Buddhas, typical examples of this, provided inspiration for the later forms both in India and beyond.

A high standard of technical and artistic efficiency was also found in the art of metal casting, notably in the colossal copper images of the Buddha. One of the best known examples is the impressive standing Buddha figure from Sultanganj, cast by cire-perdue process and assembled in sections. Another interesting feature of this period is the terracotta art portraying mostly Brahmanical divinities, found abundantly at Ahichchhatra, Basarth, Set-mahet, Rajghat, etc. These figures are evidence of a popular tradition, unaffected by scholastic and literary conventions.

H. *Fragment of Ajanta mural*

Most of the classical paintings belonging to the Gupta period have survived the ravages of time. While certain Ajanta murals which can be traced back as early as the second century B.C. have dimmed almost beyond recognition, those drawn during the late Gupta period (450-600 A.D.) are mostly intact with all their glory and grandeur. Apparently Ajanta murals depict the Jatakas, but these represent the entire force of life in terms of phenomena and romances.

The magnificence of observation, the grouping of animal life, and the composition of human figures in architectural settings found on the walls of Ajanta has been enhanced by a color work painted on a base made up of layers of mud, straw, and plaster. Skillful gradation of tone in bringing out the highlights and volume, efforts in aerial perspective, and a mastery of the relation of forms in line and color are some of the salient features of the murals of Ajanta.

The halls of Ajanta, hewn from the living rock, are planned so as to make all elements of color, form and line progress towards a climax in the central cell, which is flanked by the paintings of "Beautiful Bodhisattvas." The Buddha image is reached at last—stone brought to life in color. All storms of the human heart are silenced before it in an echo of nirvana.

No tale is told on the ceilings, which are covered with intricate geometric designs. The masters responsible for the execution of these must have been well up in interior decoration for generations. The way they have maintained unity in variety, and arranged such elements as low relief, ornamental carvings, and masses of pillars, in keeping with the architectural structures of the caves, truly speaks of their unsurpassed ability and ingenuity.

The graceful and festive damsels, the lovely paradise-dwelling *apsaras,* with fully blossomed life "bursting through the moon-breasts and wine-jar hips" are yet another scene that attracts one's wistful attention. Human from first to last, "they fly, they dance, they court, they make love unabashed."

Life in all its aspects was manifest to a high degree in these paintings and sculptures as well as in music, dance, and drama. But a formal classification and codification of almost all arts and social patterns, as evidenced through various literary works, took place during this period. The classical rigidity of the Gupta aristocracy was slowly being engulfed by a powerful mythology that steadily paved the way for a revolutionary change.

True, Buddhism as a cultural force, predominated for several centuries since the days of Asoka, but a growing movement that foreshadowed the Brahmanical revival—a return to Hinduism—determined its reorientation at almost every crucial stage.

Under the Pala dynasty in Bengal, the Mahayana form of Buddhism replaced the rigid Hinayana school, revitalizing the classical phase of Indian art for the time being, but it was only a conventionalized repetition of originally noble forms.

Buddhism had been losing its hold on the land of its birth, but its influence was profoundly felt by the world outside. Countries far beyond the Indo-Gangetic plain pulsated with inspiration, and Indian art, particularly of this period and that which followed immediately, with all its charm and dignity, found a new home in the caves at Tun Huang and Lung-men in the distant lands of Central Asia, beyond the coast line of China and Korea, in the Horyuji temple at Nara

in Japan; in the cave carvings of Bamiyan and Hadda on the borders of Afghanistan, the cities of Kashgar, Yarkand, and Khotan; in the murals of Sigiriya in Ceylon, temples of Pagan in Burma; guilded shrines of Siam and Angkor in Cambodia; again in the gigantic stupa of Borobudur in Java.

By the end of the Gupta period, it must have been evident that the "ultimate supremacy of Vedantism was only a matter of time." Buddhism was gradually losing its initiative, and sculptors were "abandoning the image of the silent and static Buddha to offer homage to more restless and dynamic deities" of Hinduism. Buddhism itself came to be more and more Brahmanical until it eventually lost its character as an independent movement, Buddha himself being assimilated into the medieval Brahmanic pantheon as the incarnation of the Hindu god Vishnu.

Aesthetically, although not realized all at once, the change effected by Brahmanism came with immense plastic possibilities in a new universe of imagery. With certain basic qualities intact in spite of apparent variations, Brahmanical art has given us a greater profusion of images and forms—now monstrous and sublime, now grotesque and delicate, abstract and sensual—than was ever attempted before by any other art.

In seeming chaos and confusion, we find in Brahmanical art a sense of broad symphonic order, a joy of rhythm. The profusion that creates an impression of bewilderment soon fades into the exuberance of nature that pervades this art. This is experienced in the Descent of the Ganges at Mahabalipuram. The large number of figures carved out of solid rock "with apparent disregard of all rational composition is seen on closer examination to radiate from and be conveyed towards a central axis in its timeless descent."

Between the profound stillness of the central head of the Mahesvaramurti of the Elephanta cave and the dynamic poise of Nataraja of South India, we have again modulations, subtle and unique, representing the most characteristic phases of the art of this period.

The sculptures of Elura cave are so full of vitality as to overwhelm the visitor at each successive step. For instance, the Kailasa temple, which is cut, carved and sculptured from virgin rock, (the artists having progressed from the top downwards), stands with all its stupendous magnificence as a unique achievement. About 200,000 tons of solid stone are known to have been removed in the chiseling out of this Siva temple.

The rhythm of Brahmanical art finds its counterpart in the economic significance of medieval feudalism. Many divergent religious thoughts and emotions coexisted and were tolerated in the broad-based social order. Sculptors reacted to these cross-currents with a futuristic adoption of many-handed figures, representing rapidity of movement and change. In the realm of plastic art we are confronted with a grandeur of conception magnificently realized in the images of Siva and Parvati, Nataraja and Ardhanarisvara, particularly of the Chola and Pallava periods. The image of Ardhanarisvara, symbolizing the union of the male and female principles that are creative without antithesis, has the poise of detached calm and yet shows all the vitality of biological existence. The symbolic representation of Nataraja, on the other hand, as the essence of cosmic transformation of energy into mass and of mass into energy, has all the rapture of bliss and realiza-

J. *Siva preforming the Dance of the Universe*

tion. The dance, as it were, manifests the eternal existence of human aspiration in the ever-changing world of space and time.

In the creation of this panorama of "gods and goddesses" the artist cared little to express his own individuality. His creation yet turned out occasionally to be a complete departure—a rare phenomenon in Indian Art. The artist never sought to immortalize himself through his art, rather in his creation he completely lost his own identity. But in these rare departures—as we find in the so-called goddess Ganga—he brings her down to the level of an earthly mortal, as it were, and gives her all the qualities and tenderness of an ordinary human being. He makes his goddess human out and out, "deep in all the heat of the pondering female blood, the female urge, the female nature," and enlivens her as a "young girl of unsurpassing loveliness."

The sculptures of this period, however, form part of the architectural design, and the temple background in which these were set had a significance of its own. Detached from this background these sculptures lose much of their meaning. That is why in a museum, without the spirit, setting, and psychology so clearly associated with them, the understanding or appreciation of Indian sculpture becomes poor and inadequate.

From the 6th century A.D., caves gave place gradually to structural temple building. The horizontal and domed tops became vertical and pointed. The vertically set sculptures not only visually increased the upward thrust of the medieval temples, but had a decorative effect "with a pronounced feeling for volume, perhaps foreshadowing a change in the medium of expression."

K. *Amorous couple from Konarak*

However, no perspective of Brahmanical art would be complete without its overpowering sensuous quality being taken into account. In the reliefs of the temples of Konarak and Khajuraho, the sensual element is developed to its logical culmination, to a point where it has almost completely shattered the aesthetic barriers and forced the ultimate realization that life is art. What is justified and fundamental in life must also be justified and fundamental in art. It is no longer a question of that "provocative indulgence" of the female figures from which Roger Fry recoils with a puritanical shudder. Here we are confronted with erotic ecstasy in all its plastic possibilities. The love-play of these images rouses a baffling query in the Western mind, but to an Indian observer the motive is simple and clear. In the world a man and a woman unite. Nothing is so true in terms of life as the after-glow of a happy union. These mating figures are drawn together in productive forces towards the creation of new life, new dynamic forms. Filled with the sense of ecstatic conviction, they are no longer torn between the contradiction of life and social existence.

These released forces militated against the interests of the ruling class, which was now strongly entrenched at the termination of the expansive phase of feudalism. A cry of artistic formalism and aesthetic injunction was therefore raised throughout the country in order to dampen and clamp down the creative movement. The result was an orgy of bombastic ornamentation and hysterical tendency towards flatulent magnificence so vivid in the temples of Mount Abu, Belur, Halebid, or in the *gopurams* (porch towers) of South India.

Art declined. And for the first time in recorded history,

India faced during this period a system of strange contrast with the advent of Islam. Out of the conflict arose problems which it was the task of Indian culture to solve. New religious and philosophical thoughts were evolved to mark the reproachment between the Hindu and Moslem outlook. After the initial impact, the Moslem ruling class ceased to be foreigners. This reaction to the Indian environment was reflected in the development of the artistic tradition of the next few centuries.

In the architecture of northern India, the general principle undergoes an almost revolutionary change. Hindu and Moslem elements merged to produce this form. Where the fusion is complete, we have brilliant architectural expression. Akbar's Fatehpur Sikri brings together these elements with the confidence of an empire builder and anticipates the more sophisticated monument where Mumtaj sleeps under the most beautiful and expensive memorial in the world. The Taj Mahal is, indeed, a wonder of architectural creation.

The painting which was brought to India by Babur, the founder of the Mughal Empire, was likewise intensely individualistic and sophisticated. It was not interested in crowds or masses. The stamp of individualism reached exaggerated lengths and reduced painting to mere portraiture, where characters "are not characters at all, but photographs out of focus." Wherever this luxury of Mughal court art came in contact with the popular tradition, it produced that sophistication which is evident in the Rajput paintings.

The mythology that once existed as a link between the economic and spiritual structures of society was no longer powerful enough to resist the unholy alliance between the ruling cliques. The result was that the indigenous vigor of

Rajput tradition was dulled by a tendency towards archaic sensuality, even sexuality, and idle romanticism, which had the patronage of the princes and emperors who were sufficiently well off to devote their leisure to the enjoyment of this art form

Even the Jain miniatures, which had long retained their boldness, also showed "the tormented outlines of faces at once nervous and sensual, representations of human beings whose passage through life is made difficult by the awareness of fears that belong to an age of conformity which is also on the threshold of the Reformation."

When individualism decayed into selfishness, the Indian artistocracy was extremely artificial and had no roots in everyday existence. The cult of beauty, art for art's sake, was practised as a form of escapism. All interests centered round the sentimental romances, which were endlessly repeated in both painting and poetry, and fictitious portraits of sultanas, begums and ranis. They were dream figures of idealized feminine beauty and accomplishment, delicately made up, decked out in the finest dresses, and over-loaded with jewelry. This cult resembled the cult of the ballerina in France of the rococo period, when kings and princes lay at the feet of the adored.

But out of the dead remains of these court splendors there finally arose a cultural awakening of the Indian masses. This was a period of constant revolt against the conventional fetters of social and religious ideas. Chandidas, the greatest popular composer of Padavali songs, declared in the fifteenth century: "Listen, O brother man, the Truth of Man is the highest of truth; there is no other truth above it."

Gods tremble before men, ready to do the biddings of the

L. *Tribal art: simple yet bold*

peasant, to plow his field, harvest his crop, and carry it to his home. A large number of newly discovered folk paintings portray the real conditions of people's life at that time, and every one of these paintings is a condemnation of the social injustice. At the bottom of each scroll there are always scenes of Hell depicting every imaginable torture to which all antisocial elements are subjected in punishment of their worldly sins. In order to leave no doubt in the popular mind about the real meaning of these paintings, explanatory songs composed by the artists themselves always accompanied the public unrolling of the scrolls.

Their usual themes are street scenes, popular folklore, festivals and family reunions, the joys and sorrows of everyday life together with biting satires on the vices of the decaying social order. Apart from its simple technique, Indian folk art by its nature and function, has useful lessons for creative artists in search of basic forms.

It is not a coincidence that the same basic forms run through the artistic expression of the few surviving tribes who still maintain a more or less primitive way of life. The plastic freedom has been kept alive in the wood carvings of Maria Gond tribes of Bastar State and particularly among the Nagas of Eastern India. The mind which expresses itself in direct simplicity and vigor of primitive art was poignantly brought out when a Naga youth, asked about his trouble, replied at once: "Whenever I love a girl, she immediately becomes pregnant." The thrust of his chisel has the same certainty and boldness.

Until recently nobody has taken the trouble of recording the artistic tradition of these people. The impact of Europe brought in an entirely new set of conditions which upset the social basis of primitive and folk art tradition of India. Even a century ago, the life of the guild artist was closely integrated in the economic life of the village. In exchange for his art products the artist was assigned a measure of land by the village community for his maintenance. Thus the other party to the deal was the collective organization of the village, and the artist was primarily an artist of the people. But with the break-up of the economic life of the villages that followed the British rule, the indigenous arts and crafts were not only seriously threatened but destroyed in many parts of the country.

The Europeans who came to India had no intention of settling here and were not really interested in a cultural synthesis between the East and the West. It was as if two closed systems faced each other and were not prepared either to influence or to imbibe anything from the contact. Nor was there any attempt to build up a new integration though there were sporadic efforts by a few western scholars who had been dazzled by the splendor of Indian civilization. The spirit of European art on the other hand could not be successfully assimilated by the Indian artists in their blind imitation. The result was Ravi Varma, whose syrupy pictures were an extreme example of philistine perversity.

But the period of fake European tradition did not last long. The wave of reformism, particularly in Bengal, needed a new vehicle of artistic expression. The rising Indian bourgeoisie took to classicism which was introduced by Abanindranath Tagore and carried all over India by his students. The outcome of this movement is well known as Bengal School of Art in which the name of Nandalal Bose stands out. He

м. *" Head," by Jamani Roy*

depicted the mythological stories in the traditional technique of the Ajanta mural paintings. The enthusiasm for antiquity was surely the ideological reflection of the struggle over the choice of technique, western or eastern. The enthusiasm continued until the economic crisis of World War I, which sharpened the Indian national movement and led to the growth of mass organizations, and brought new trends. All the artifices of the old school, now of no use to any class, were no longer appropriate to the aspirations and aesthetic tendencies produced by the modern social relationships.

In the period that followed, Rabindranath Tagore took up painting. Inspired by modern thought and technique, the daring experiment of Tagore marks the final break with the sentimental love of artistic revivalism. The dramatic appearance of Jamini Roy as a popular artist is a direct outcome of this departure. Today the name of Jamini Roy can be placed side by side with those of Cezanne, Picasso or Matisse. Like many who have broken with conventions in their quest for new sources of inspiration, Jamini Roy is sustained by the art of the people, which is ageless and universal.

The Arts of India: MAP

In India we find during every period when her civilization bloomed, an intense joy in life and nature, a pleasure in the act of living, the development of art and music and literature and song and dancing and painting and the theatre, and even a highly sophisticated inquiry into sex relations.

JAWAHARLAL NEHRU

TUN-HUANG

KOREA

JAPAN

NARA

BET

LHASA

C H I N A

PAGAN

BURMA

NGAL

SIAM

BANGKOK

ANGKOR

CAMBODIA

PHNOMPENH

PHILIPPINES

SUMATRA

BORNEO

JAVA

BOROBUDUR

PRAMBANAM

Map 37

The Arts of India: PLATES

NOTE: THE CHRONOLOGY IS ON A FOLD-OUT
FLAP OPPOSITE THE LAST PLATE. THIS FEATURE
ALLOWS THE READER TO CONSULT IT AT THE
SAME TIME HE IS LOOKING AT THE PLATES.

§ 1 Hunting Scene
Singanpur / Rock painting, mauve, pale yellow & burgundy / End Old Stone Age

Some drawings here represent men and animals gripped in intense struggle. It is difficult to assume whether or not the drawings had magical significance.

§ 2 Wounded Boar
Mirzapur / Rock painting, mauve, pale yellow & burgundy / End Old Stone Age

The boar shows the agony of death and early man's triumph over his adversaries in the animal world. The modeling of the form has added considerably to the esthetic value.

§ 4 DOLMENS
Reichur / Old Stone Age
A diversified primitive culture had already emerged in India during prehistoric times and created striking forms, the impact of which has been felt in India throughout the ages. Old and new stone aged finds, especially in the Godavari and Narmada cultures, are almost identical to Aurignacian, Magdalenian and Azilian types.

§ 3 HORSERIDER
Engraved on rock shelter wall / Near Baretha Dar Falls, Bharatpur / Old Stone Age
Depicting the animal with open mouth and bending legs, the artist has intended to create a state of agitation. Numerous other examples of such rock engraving have been found at different places in India, but the historical sequence of these and rock paintings is still an unsolved problem.

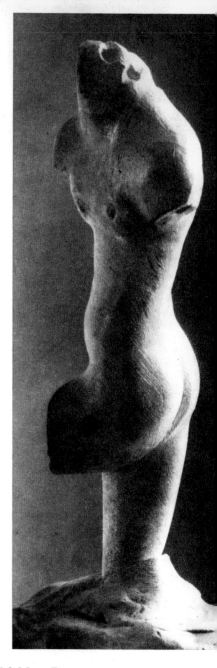

§ 5 MALE TORSO
Harappa / Red limestone / 9 *cm* high
3000–2000 B.C. / National Museum,
New Delhi
Extraordinarily exact in anatomical detail, this male torso shows both volume and suppleness. Its style foreshadows later Indian sculpture and painting, especially that of the Mauryan age. A main feature of the technique is the socketing of head and arms. The nipples were cemented on.

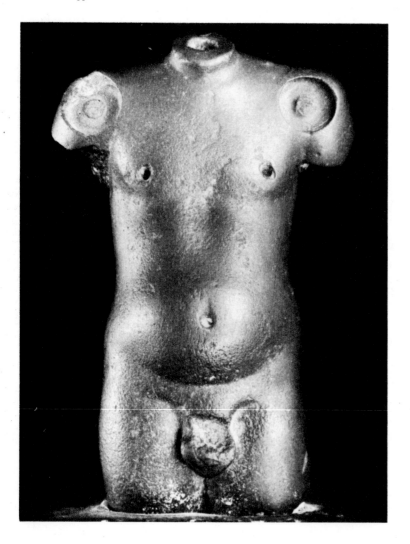

§ 6 MALE DANCER
Harappa / Grey limestone / 10 *cm* high
3000–2000 B.C.
National Museum, New Delhi
With the body twisting and the left leg thrown out, this figure shows the sculptor's mastery over his material. The head, arms, and genitals, now missing, were socketed into the torso. The nipples were cemented on.

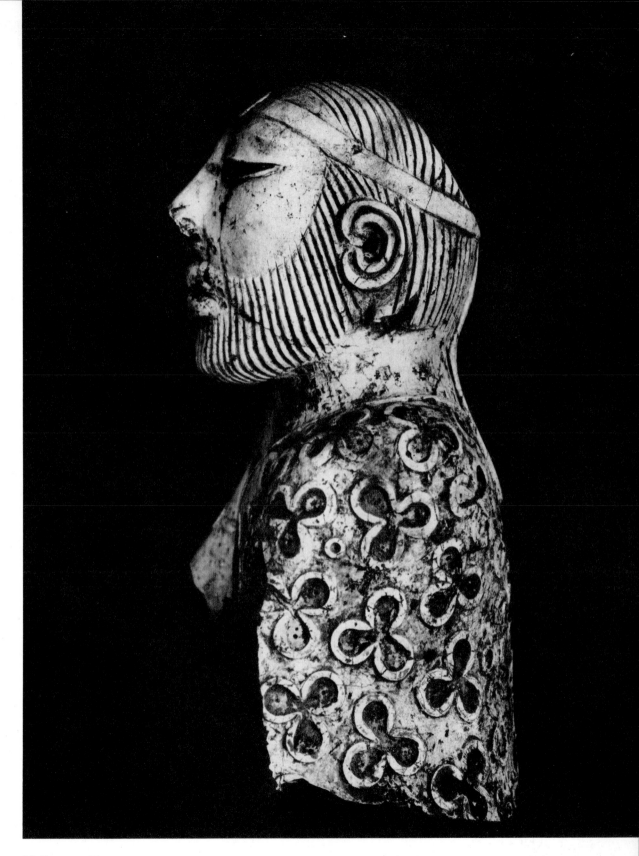

§ 7 IMAGE OF PRIEST
Mohenjo-daro / Alabaster / 18 *cm* / 3,000–2,000 B.C.
National Museum, Karachi
*A man wearing a trifoil ornamented robe. It may portray
a priest,* guru, *or god.*

§ 8 & § 9 Figurines
Mohenjo-daro / Terracotta / 3,000–2,000 B.C.
5 to 8 cm / National Museum, New Delhi
These figurines have the impress of ageless types which persist over the years in varied forms—virgins, animals, mother-child figures predominate. Heads are usually pitcher shaped (kalasa) and sometimes finished with a spade or fan-like chura. The eyes are affixed, incised or indented—some have no mouth at all and on others it is only suggested. In these Indus Valley terracottas, generally formed by pinching and pelleting, the nose is prominent and the eyes are round, separately affixed and sometimes pierced. Necklaces and girdles decorate otherwise nude female figurines.

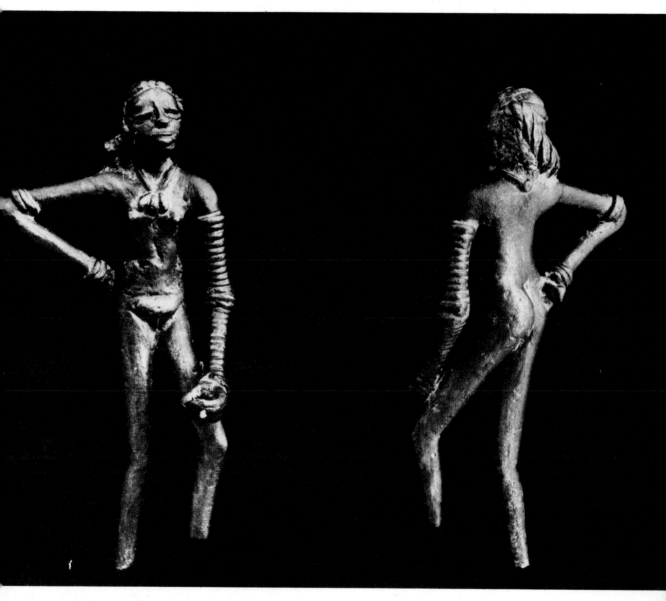

§ 10 Dancing Girl (front and rear views)
Mohenjo-daro / Bronze / 9 *cm* high / 3000–2000 B.C.
National Museum, New Delhi
*One of the earliest examples of cire-perdue metal
casting in India. The style represents another facet
of the Indus Valley tradition.*

§ 11 Bull Seal (impression)
Mohenjo-daro / Seal made of steatite / 3.8 × 3.8 cm
3000–2000 B.C. / National Museum, New Delhi
The intaglioed seals show extremely advanced craftsmanship.
The conceptual presentation of the bull indicates connections
with Mesopotamia. The pictograph at the top is yet un-
deciphered. Note the actual size of the impression.

§ 12 Yogi Seal (impression)
Mohenjo-daro / Seal made of steatite
3,000–2,000 B.C.
National Museum, New Delhi
The six-faceted god Kartikeya surrounded
by six animals is seated in the yogi
pose (paryankabandha asana).

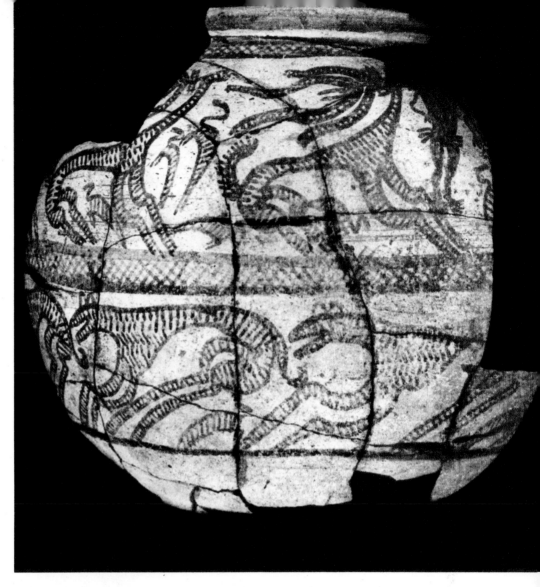

§ 13 Painted Pottery
Aurangabad, Daimabad excavation, 38 *cm* high
2,000 B.C. / Coll. of Antiquities, Safdarjang
With decoration consisting of two horizontal panels
divided by a thick border of criss-crossed lines,
this object is representative of prehistoric art in
South India. Animals show a tendency to whirl-like
movement, which here is emphasized by the deer
antlers (top row).

§ 14 Nude
Lauriya-Nandangarth / Embossed gold plaque
2.5 *cm* high / *c.* 800 B.C. / Indian Museum, Calcutta
Found in a burial casket, this figure probably represents
the earth goddess. It serves as a link between the art of the
Indus and Ganges Valleys. The organization of the form
reminds one of the Vedic concept of units of measurement.

§ 15 Lɪᴏɴ Cᴀᴘɪᴛᴀʟ
Sarnath / Polished Sandstone
322–185 ʙ.ᴄ. / Sarnath Museum
*One of the monolithic capitals from high memorial
columns erected by Asoka to the glory and propagation
of Buddhism. Here four rather stiff lions face the
cardinal points while less formal horses prance at the
base in between representations of the Wheel of the Law.*

§ 16 Bᴜʟʟ Cᴀᴘɪᴛᴀʟ
Rampurva / Sandstone / 202.5 *cm* high
322–185 ʙ.ᴄ. / Rashtrapati Bhavan, New Delhi
*This monolithic capital of highly polished stone portrays
the traditional Indian bull with all its restrained
vigor and dignity. In style it is much closer to
traditional Indian sculpture than the Lion Capital.*

§ 18 WEEPING WOMAN
Sarnath / Sandstone fragment / 2nd c. B.C.
Sarnath Museum
*Her ancient grief is revealed in hard stone
through the bent head, hidden face, and the
sensitive curve of the body.*

17 YAKSHI
Didarganj / Sandstone / 160 *cm* high
nd c. B.C. / Patna Museum, Bihar
*Suggesting a long-established tradition,
his superb figure of a dryad (of Hindu
rigin) has few Indian parallels in spirit
r execution. Massive and sensuous, with
irm legs, curving hips, narrow waist and a
eeply hollowed navel, with solid but resilient,
trong and adult bosoms, broad shoulders
nd a luminous facial expression, she is
he very embodiment of a classic beauty.*

§ 19 HEAD
Sarnath / Sandstone / 15 *cm* high / 300 c. B.C.
National Museum, New Delhi
*Probably a donor's portrait. The wide eyes,
heavy lips, and long, curly moustache give
the head an expression of massiveness. The
surface of the stone is highly polished.*

§ 20 YAKSHI
       (CHULAKOKA DEVATA)
Bharhut / Red sandstone
212 *cm* high / 185–80 B.C.
Indian Museum, Calcutta
Standing on an elephant, executing the latavestitaka *tree embrace, the massive yakshi reveals the primitive vigor characteristic of Bharhut art.*

§ 21 Yakshi (Chandra)
Bharhut / Red sandstone / 215 *cm* high
185–80 B.C. / Indian Museum, Calcutta
*This yakshi shares with the one in plate 20
massive quality and vigor. The highly ornate
headdress, sensitive face, and well-modeled
limbs mark an advance in stone sculpture.
The vehicle (vahana) on which she stands is
here not an elephant but a fish-tailed horse.*

38. (5).
b.

§ 22 YAKSHA (KUVERA)
Barhut / Red sandstone / 212 *cm* high
185–80 B.C. / Indian Museum, Calcutta
With folded hands Kuvera, king of the
dryads, reveals the primitive vigor that
is characteristic of the art of Bharhut.
This figure is from the corner of a
railing pillar.

§ 23 MAYA'S DREAM
Bharhut / Red sandstone / 51 *cm* high
185–80 B.C. / Indian Museum, Calcutta
This scene from a railing medallion shows
in low relief the conception of the Buddha.
The event occurred during a dream in which
Maya, the future mother of the Great Being,
dreams that a white elephant enters her womb.
The carving technique suggests a centuries-
old tradition of wood sculpture before
stone came into play.

§ 24 WORSHIP OF THE BODHI TREE
Barhut / Red Sandstone / 51 *cm* high
185–80 B.C. / Indian Museum, Calcutta
The Bodhi tree, under which the Buddha
attained enlightenment, is shown, but the
Buddha is conspicuous by his absence. In
this age his presence is indicated, by symbols
such as the Lotus, the Wheel of the Law,
or by the Blessed Footprints, On the other
hand, the world of the senses is portrayed
in powerful narrative style.

Sunga Dynasty 55

§ 25 Sanchi, North Gate (below)

§ 26 Sanchi, East Gate (right)
Sanchi, stupa I / Sandstone / about 10.5 *m* high / 70–25 B.C.
Bigger than the stupa of Bharhut and larger than previous
stupas at Sanchi, this Buddhist memorial offered the popular
arts great expression in the stone railings and gateways.
Much of the technique is borrowed from the ivory carver.
Stories of the Buddha are told in continuous narration. The
Yakshis, which serves as bracket figures (detail, right) on
the gateways seem to be ideal female forms as conceived
in the India of that age.

§ 27 CHAITYA VERANDAH

Karli / Rock-cut facade / Late 1st c. A.D.
*This rock-cut temple, chiseled out of stone in
the nature of wooden construction, reflects an
older tradition of temples made of less durable
materials. The façade, whose "wooden ribs"
can be seen, offers a perfect equilibrium of
design and dimension from every angle, and
each carving or opening is relevant to it. The
figures, niches, and double arches create an
impression of upward thrust and mobility.
The detail in* plate 28 *(right) can be seen at
the left of the chaitya entrance.*

§ 28 DONOR COUPLE
(DETAIL OF PLATE 27)

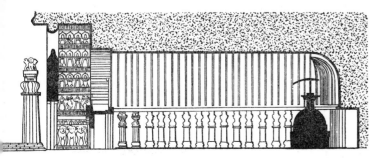

N. *Chaitya at Karli (see* plate 27)

§ 29 Cave I (left)

§ 30 Chaitya Caves, general view
Guntapalle / Rock cut / *c* 2nd c. b.c.
*Here (as in plate 17) the façades of the chaitya
halls reflect the forms of wooden architectural
structures. Completely cut from the living rock,
these structures housed the monks of the ever-
growing Buddhist religion.*

§ 31 Interior, Cave I

*This partial view of the stupa and ceiling, as well as
the sketch on page 59, show the structure of
the figure part of a chaitya. The umbrella and other
decorative elements are missing from the stupa, but the
sketch illustrates this and the uses of columns.*

§ 32 Yakshi

Mathura / Red sandstone / 129 cm high
2nd c. A.D. / Indian Museum, Calcutta

*This superb figure in the Yakshi tradition at
first appears to be nude, but the ridge across
her feet indicates a diaphanous muslin skirt.
She carries a bird cage while a parrot pecks
at her hair. The significance of the dwarf on
which she stands is not definitely known. On
the balcony above two women are engaged
in toilet.*

§ 33 Goose Girl

Begram / Ivory carving / 7.5 cm high / c 200 A.D.
Kabul Museum

*Following in the tradition of Mathura, a group of
artists, probably from India, founded a great art
center near Kabul. They were not only masters in
shaping ivory, but were equally efficient in carving
rock boulders into images of colossal dimension.*

§ 34 IMAGE OF BUDDHA
Bodhgaya / Sandstone / c 4th c. A.D.
National Museum, New Delhi
This image of the Buddha, done in the
distinctly Indian style of Mathura, is
seated cross-legged in the padmasana
yogi posture.

§ 35 Head
Taxila / Stucco / 27 cm high / 2nd–3rd c. B.C.
Indian Museum, Calcutta
*Though under the Kushan conquerors of Central
Asia, this head shows the influence of Greece
and Rome at work in Gandhara. Art here developed
into a vigorous local Indian school. The delicate
handling of the features are characteristic of
much of the art of Gandhara.*

§ 36 Head of the Buddha
Gandhara / Stucco / c 3rd–4th c. A.D.
Indian Museum, Calcutta
*Regardless of whether the earliest re-
presentations of the Buddha in other than
symbolic form first occurred at Gandhara
or Mathura, the style of Gandhara bears
little relation to that of sculpture in India
proper.*

§ 37 Seated Buddha
Gandhara / Stucco / c 3rd c. A.D.
Indian Museum, Calcutta
A typical Gandhara Buddha in a yogi pose.

§ 38 Sujata and the Naga of the Mango Ferry
Nagarjunakonda / Stone / *c* 2nd c. A.D.
*Representative of the Amarativati style is
this depicition of a scene from the life of
the Buddha.*

§ 39 BUDDHA AND THE MUST ELEPHANT
Stupa I, Amaravati / Grey marble / 80 *cm* high
150–300 A.D. / Government Museum, Madras
A remarkable scene from a story of an attempt on
the life of the Buddha by his evil cousin, Devadatta.
In a two part picture, the Must (wild) elephant sent to
kill the Buddha first enters the gate and creates panic
among the citizens. Women on the balcony watch
in silent horror as the elephant reaches the Buddha,
only to bow down in submission before the Master.

§ 40 STANDING BUDDHA (NEXT PAGE)
Mathura / Red sandstone / 217 *cm* high
320–500 A.D. / Rashtrapati Bhavan, New Delhi
Standing in benign majesty, Buddha asks the
world not to fear. The position of the broken
right arm suggests that it was held in the
Abhaya mudhra, one of many hand poses with
symbolic meaning. The Abaya mudhra is
a sign to quell fear.

§ 41 SEATED BUDDHA
Sarnath / Sandstone / 219 cm high / c 5th c. A.D.
Sarnath Museum, Banaras
In this fully evolved Buddha image, the Master is shown preaching the First Sermon in the Deer Bark of Banaras.

§ 42 INDRA & CELESTIALS (PRECEDING PAGE)
Ajanta, cave XVII / Mural / 320–500 A.D.
These characters from Hindu legend show Gupta art at its zenith as well as showing Mahayana Buddhism at its most cosmopolitan. Soon Buddhism will fade from the Indian scene. At Ajanta the artist has created wonders in depth, dimension and color, using pigments mainly from rock and vegetable sources.

§ 43 MALE FIGURE (PRECEDING PAGE)
Ajanta, cave I / Mural detail / 320–500 A.D.
Part of a scene from the Champaye Jataka, one
of the tales of former lives of the Buddha.

§ 44 AVALOKITESVARA PADMAPANI (ABOVE)
Ajanta, cave I, Mural detail / 320–500 A.D.

§ 45 FEMALE CHAURI BEARER (RIGHT)
Ajanta, cave I / Mural detail / 320–500 A.D.

§ 46   FIGHTING BULLS
Ajanta, cave I / Mural, detail / 600 A.D.
A masterpiece of animal study in the later Gupta style.
Working in light reflected through a white muslin placed
outside the large dark halls, the guild artist of Ajanta
expressed new ideas using ancient methods and techniques.

§ 47 Ajanta Caves I–IXX
Ajanta / Rock-cut caves
2nd c. b.c.–7th c. a.d.

§ 48 Musicians from the Temptation Panel
Ajanta, cave XXVI / Rock carving / 400–642 a.d.
In rock no less than in pigment, the Indian artist
created figures full of life and sensual charm.

§ 49 DWARPALA (DOORKEEPER)
Ajanta, cave II / Rock carving / 400–642 A.D.

§ 50   LADY WITH LOTUS
Sigiriya / Mural, detail / 479–497 A.D.
This figure, holding a blossoming flower in
one hand and two lotuses and a water lily in the
other, is said to be a court lady of a Ceylonese king.
The style and purity of line show Gupta influence

§ 51 Parvati
Ahichchhatra / Terracotta / 12 *cm* high
500 A.D. / National Museum, New Delhi
*Revealing the ideal of feminine beauty of
the times is this head of the Hindu goddess
Parvati, consort of the god Siva.*

§ 52 The Boar Avatar of Vishnu
Udayagiri / Rock sculpture / *c* 5th c. A.D
*The ten incarnations of the god Vishnu explain the various
states of evolution. In his third incarnation, Vishnu mani-
fested himself as a boar in order to rescue the earth, which
was submerged under the ocean of non-existence.*

§ 53 Columns
Indra Sabha Cave, Elura / Rock hewn
600–850 A.D.
Under the chisel of Indian artists, even rocks
flowered into beautiful forms. These columns
from Hindu cave-temples were evolved beyond
their utilitarian purpose with decorative
ornamentation.

§ 54 Embracing Couple
Kailasa Temple, Elura
Rock hewn / 600–850 A.D.
*Carved in deep relief, this union
of male and female is a symbol
of eternal consumation. He is
erect and motionless, as if in
possession of the darkest and
most secret depths of her being.*

§ 55 Dancing Female Figure
Aurangabad, cave VII / Rock sculpture
c 7th c. A.D.
*Though cut from stone the thin, filmy garment
clings realistically to the dancing figure.*

§ 57 Visvakarman Cave Facade
Elura cave / Rock cut / *c* 700–750 A.D.
Called Visvakarman, or "Lord of the Arts"
this cave shows a rather baroque style when
compared to the chaitya facades in plates 27,
30 & 31. *The figures are flying heavenly*
beings.

§ 58 DESCENT OF THE GANGES
Mahabalipuram / Rock hewn / 600–750 A.D.
*Indian artists, undaunted by the unwieldy material,
have created on a giant boulder this monumental frieze
depicting gods, men, and animals offering thanks to Siva
for the Ganges river. All of the figures, including the
elephants, are life size in this lyrical combination of
naturalism and symbolism. The center cleft represents
the river coming down from the Himalayas, and at one
time actual water flowed through this channel.*

§ 59, § 60 & § 61 DESCENT OF THE GANGES
*At right is a figure of Bhagiratha seated before
a shrine worshipping Siva (the shrine is visible
in plate 58, lower left). The deer, below, show the
heights which animal sculpture attained in India.
The figures on the opposite page are devas (gods)
and holy men, all paying homage to Siva for the
gift of the Ganges to India. All figures are life
size.*

§ 62 Figure of Woman
Madhya Pradesh / Sandstone
89 *cm* high / 6th or 7th c. A.D.
Indian Museum, Culcutta
*This fragment is painted red. This
gracefully carved figure whose
lower body is covered by a thin
garment, stands on a cornice on
which a lizard is carved.*

63 WOMAN WITH PARROT
Rajmahal
Whitish Sandstone
6th or 7th c. A.D.
Patna Museum, Bihar

*Framed by rosette borders, this
figure is carved in deep relief
as if in a doorway. She
appears to be feeding the bird.
Her thin garment is similar to
the one in the preceding plate.*

§ 64 & § 65 THREE-HEADED MAHESA
Siva Temple, Elephanta / Rock hewn / 360 *cm* high / 8th c. A.D.
The Mahesa, or Siva Trinity, is a dramatic representation of
the supreme form of Siva as the center face, Siva as destroyer
at left, and on the right, Parvati, the wife. The detail below shows
the central face in profile. This trinity is the climax of many
carvings concerned with Siva, and the pose of the figures in
meditation, no less than the setting in a dark niche, suggest
mystery and power while symbolizing the union of the inner self
with the cosmic world.

§ 66 FEMALE FIGURE
Nagesvarswami Temple, Kumbhokonam / Bold relief
c 8th C. A.D.

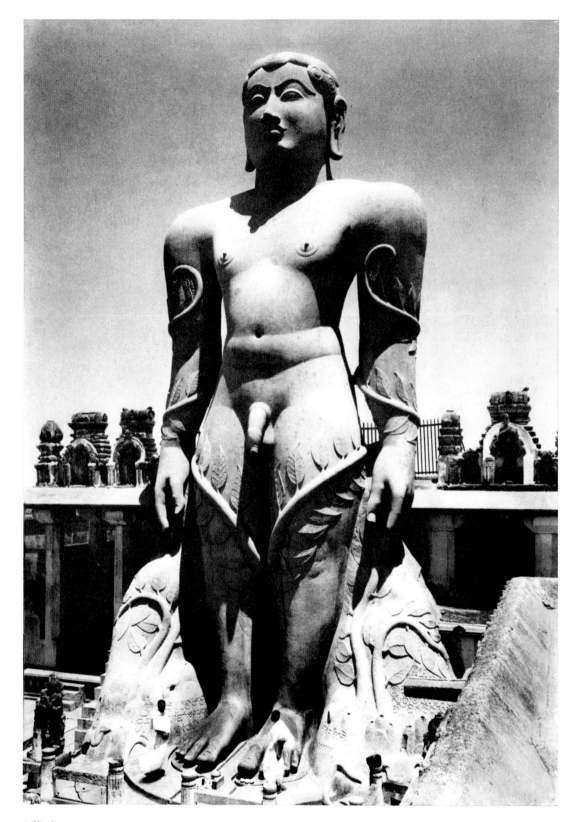

§ 67 GOMMATESVARA

Sravana Belgola / Stone / 17.38 *m* high / 10th c. A.D.

This colossus, the biggest monolithic statue in the world,
stands as a great sentinel, majestic and severe, between
earth and sky. The vines represent those said to have
grown up around this Jaina saint during the year in which
he stood in this position engaged in deep meditation. The
technique shows exceptional comprehension of form and
volume in the human body.

§ 68 TORANA (GATE)
Muktesvara Temple, Bhubanesvara
Sandstone / *c* 950 A.D.
*A singular architectural triumph of the ancient
Hindu in arch construction is this gate, whose
massive supports give an effect of solidity that
is effectively counterbalanced by the decorative
motifs at the top and base.*

§ 69 GABAKSHA
Muktesvara Temple, Bhabanesvara
Sandstone / *c* 950 A.D.
A combination of ornamental designs
plus human and animal figures, with
the stress on pure patterns, make up
this detail from a Hindu temple.

§ 70 FIGURE OF SUDHANA
Borobudur, gallery 1 / Volcanic stone
750 A.D.
*Carved in pitted volcanic rock, a most
unsympathetic material, these reliefs,
Indian influence in faraway
Borobudur, Java, tell stories of the life
of the Buddha (plate 68) and also illustrate
Jatakas—stories of the Buddha in his
previous incarnations. Here Prince
Sudhana casts his ring into the waterpot
of one of the Kinnaris at the fountain,
while others of the tribe return home.*

§ 71 SUJATA'S OFFERING
Borobudur
Volcanic stone / 750 A.D.
*Sujata, daughter of an outcast,
offers the Buddha the first morsel
of food he takes after his years
of intense meditation. The temples
of Borobudur are covered with
endless bas-reliefs showing how
readily accepted Buddhism was
in Southeast Asia.*

§ 73 BODHISATTVA
Horyuji Temple, Nara / mural detail
8th c. A.D.
*This portion of a mural (tragically lost
in a fire 1949) was part of the Golden
Hall (Kondo) of the Horyuji in Japan's
ancient capital. The influence of India
is evident, if not the hand of an Indian
artist, in this figure of a Buddhist deity.*

§ 72 WATER NYMPH
Dandan U'iliq / Mural, detail / *c* 8th c. A.D.
*Central Asia was the fusion ground of various
influences from the great civilizations around.
Indian influence was especially strong at the
site where this female figure is painted. Central
Asia was also the gate through which Indian culture,
mainly in the form of Buddhism, passed into China.*

§ 74 Lingaraja Temple
Bhubanesvara / Sandstone / 43.2 *m* high
c 1000 A.D.

The many Hindu temples near Bhubanesvara
are the chief monuments of the Orissan school,
with this one generally considered the finest.
It shows towers representative in shape of the
final stage of North Indian style. A tremendous
force seems to drive the structure upwards,
creating an impression of movement in space.

§ 75 WOMAN WRITING WITH A STYLUS
Khajuraho / Sandstone / 70 *cm* high
c 950–1050 A.D. / Indian Museum, Calcutta
One of many female figures that adorn the
temples at Khajuraho. They show a sensuous
awareness of the human form and are out-
standing works in the long tradition of female
sculpture in India.

§ 76 SALABHANJIKA
Khajuraho / Sandstone / *c* 950–1050 A.D.
Indian Museum, Calcutta
A classical attitude of tree-goddesses in
Indian art.

§ 77 & § 78 Kandariya Mahadeva Temple
Khajuraho / Sandstone / 30 m high / 950–1050 A.D.
*This temple to Siva is representative of Central Indian architecture,
showing a more unified, organic overall shape. Built on a terrace,
the horizontal stability balances the vertical mobility of the tower
(sikhara). The massive groupings are intersected by the main lines,
shadows, and porches. The base is crowded by diverse figures, but
inside the temple where one meditates, it is plain and dark—the
darkness of the womb. (see also plate 81, color)*

§ 79 SURASUNDARI
Visvan the Temple, Khajuraho / Sandstone / 950–1050 A.D.

§ 80 Kandariya Mahadeva Temple
(see captions, plates 77 & 78)

§ 81 Nayika (FEMALE FIGURE)
Lingaraja Temple, Bhubanesvara / Sandstone
c 1000 A.D.

§ 82 Nayika (female figure)
Rajasthan / Sandstone / *c* 12th c. A.D.
Villiers David Coll., London

§ 83 CYMBAL PLAYER
Surya Deul Temple, Konarak / Sandstone
1240–1280 A.D.

§ 84 VRISHABHAVAHANAMURTI WITH DEVI (FACING PAGE)
Tiruvengadu, Tanjavur / Bronze / 106.5 cm high
& 93 cm high / 1011 A.D. / Tanjavur Art Gallery
Siva and his consort done during the early Chola dynasty.

§ 85 Siva as Lord of the Dance
(Natarja)
Tiruvelangadu / Bronze / 114.5 *cm* high
11th c. A.D. / Government Museum,
Madras

*Siva, engaged in the dance of the universe,
tramples on the dwarf of illusion, while
holding the drum of creation in the upper
right hand and the fire of destruction in the
corresponding left. The lower right hand is
stretched out in a gesture of protection (abhaya),
and the lower left signifies salvation. The
outer ring of fire symbolizes the universe.
A unique blend of poise and movement, this
sculpture is remarkable for the balance of
the limbs and the rhythm running through them.*

§ 86 Lion Bracket
Khajuraho / Sandstone / 108 *cm* high
11th c. A.D. / National Museum, New Delhi

*The treatment of the lion, whose human rider
is so small as to be almost invisible, is highly
stylized. The left hind leg of the beast is about
to come down on a warrior who is twisting in
a final desperate movement to defend himself.*

§ 87 & § 88 Mithuna (union)
Jagadamba Temple, Khajuraho
Sandstone
180 *cm* high / 1059–1087 A.D.
Two stages of union are depicted in these figures. Right, the female surrenders as the lover removes the outer garment. At left, the figures are interlocked in their embrace. These frankly erotic scenes represent the drawing together of productive forces towards the creation of new life, new dynamic forms.

§ 89, § 90 & § 91 Surya Deul (Temple of the Sun)
Konarak / Sandstone / 26.18 × 173.73 *m*
1240–1280 A.D.

*The tallest remaining portion of this great temple is
the assembly hall, the tower being in ruins. The overall form is a huge chariot—the chariot of the sun—with
great eight-spoked wheels (the divisions of the day and
night). The symbolic figures on the spokes seem to move
as one passes by. From the base to the top of the temple,
life is depicted in all its variety and immensity. No phase,
including the sensual, is ignored.*

*From a distance, the eye is tilted to embrace it; then
it is caught by a succession of structural lines and
ultimately brought to rest by the circular* amlaka *(top
ornament), and the base—a pure composition, rare in
Indian architecture.*

§ 92 MITHUNA
Surya Deul Temple, Konarak / Sandstone
1240–1280 A.D.
These interlocked figures are rendered with a rare
combination of monumental and mobile qualities—
breathing of flesh and feeling, and through convulsed
curves portray the desire for a total sinking of self
at the moment of mating. But the whole impression
makes one forget the real theme and suggests the
idea of some mysterious underlying purpose.

§ 93 SURYA
Surya Deul Temple, Konarak / Chlorite
240 *cm* high / 1240–1280 A.D.
The sun god is depicted with Dandin, the
dispenser of justice on his right and Pingala,
the recorder of human deeds on the left.
The former holds a sword and the latter,
a pen and ink pot.

§ 94 Elephant and Warrior
Surya Deul Temple, north gate
Sandstone / 1240–1280 A.D.
*The elephant carries a warrior in his trunk.
This sympathetic study of animal life is full
of the same spirit that inspired the early
sculpture of Bharhut and Sanchi.*

§ 95 Cymbal Player
Surya Deul Temple, Konarak
Sandstone / 1240–2180 A.D.
*Placed high up on successive pyramidal
tiers, bold and gay figures of female
musicians such as this show that religion
did not inhibit the Indian artist.*

§ 96 Female Torso
Konarak / Sandstone
1240–1280 A.D.
Konarak Museum, Orissa

§ 97 Ardhanarisvara
Vikrampur / Black stone / 12th c. A.D.
Dacca Museum, Bengal
This figure represents both Siva and his
wife, Parvati, in one body. The male and
female attributes are each shown in this
divine union—a symbol of primal creation
and, united, they become the most powerful
force unfolding divergent aspects of cosmic
reality.

§ 98 Ganga (above)
Rajsahi / Black stone / 170 cm high
12th c. A.D. / V.R.S. Museum, Rajsahl
*In elaborate attire and costly ornaments,
this figure could very well be the portrait
of a full-blooded woman of the age, though
in fact the figure is a goddess.*

§ 99 Vishnu & Attendant
Sundarban, 24 Parganas / Copper Plate engraving
20.5×27 cm / 1198 A.D. / Asutosh Museum, Calcutta
*A land grant inscription with silver coating. The lines,
with their lyrical grace, approximate the trend of
medieval painting. The style greatly influenced art
in Southeast Asia, particularly that of Indonesia.*

§ 100 Scene from the Jatakas
Payathonzu Temple, Pagan / Mural detail
13th c. A.D.
*The nervous outline of these murals shows
stylistic affinities with the medieval paintings
of Bengal. Characteristic features are the
three-quarter view of the face and the
elongated eyes and nose.*

§ 101 AMBIKA (SEE FOLLOWING PAGES)
Tejapala Temple, Mount Abu / White Marble / 1232 A.D.
This detail shows how at Mt. Abu the marble was scraped rather than chipped, resulting in a mechanical perfection.

§ 102 Frieze
Tejapala Temple, Mt. Abu

§ 103 Ceiling
Tejapala Temple, Mount Abu
The ceiling of this Jaina temple, built high
on Mt. Abu, represents a mandala (cosmic
diagram) with its concentric circles. The
scraping method used on the marble mars
the total effect, and the exuberance of the
total decor obscures the structural form of
the building.

§ 104 Female Bracket Figure
Ramappa Temple, Palampet / Stone / *c* 12th c. A.D.

§ 105 Madanika (a celestial being)
Chenna Kesava Temple, Belur / Stone
12th c. a.d.

In this figure bracket, one of thirty-eight that decorate the capitals of the pillars, the ornaments add to the feeling of rhythm by modifying the thrusts of torso and limbs.

§ 106 & § 107 Jain Tirthankaras
Gwalior / Carved in cliffs / *c* 15th c. A.D.
*These figures of saints (trithankars) of the
Jain religion show the interesting turn that
much Jain sculpture takes in contrast to some
which is almost identical to much of Buddhist
and Hindu sculpture.*

§ 108 GWALIOR FORT
Gwalior / Stone and brick / c 1500 A.D.
Decorative details show Mughal influence
in this large fort.

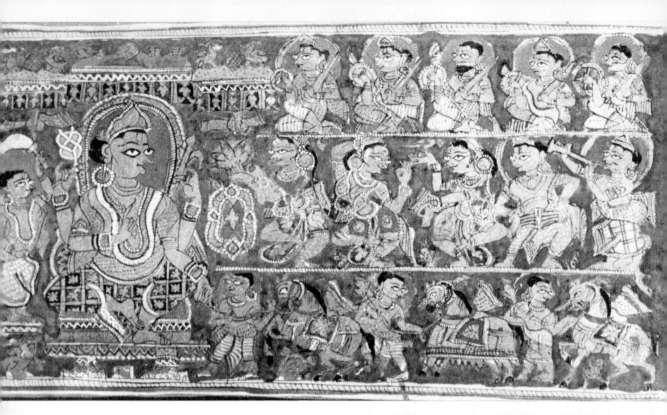

§ 109 ILLUSTRATION OF JAIN MANUSCRIPT
Western India / Painting on paper
c 14th C. A.D. / Bharat Kala Bhavan, Banaras

§ 110 THE HEROINE ADORED BY HER MAID
Eastern India / Painting on paper
19 × 11 *cm* / Bharat Kala Bhavan, Banaras

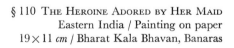

§ 111 PARVATI
Tanjavur, Madras / Bronze / 66 *cm* high
c 14th C. A.D. / Gautam Sarabhai Coll., Ahmedabad
One of countless statues of the consort of Siva.

§ 112 SITA
Madras (provenance unknown) / Bronze
17–18th C. A.D. / 96.5 *cm* high
Cowasji Jehangir Coll., Bombay
Another consort of a god, this one of
Rama's (an incarnation of Vishnu) wife.

§ 113 PANCH MAHAL
Fetehpur Sikri / Red sandstone / 16th c. A.D.
*This five-storied pavilion of Akbar's time is an
example of how Hindu and Islamic craftsmanship
fused in India. The ground floor, adorned profusely
by vigorous columns, was subdivided into thin screens
of stone, some perforated, some solid.*

§ 114 AKBAR'S TOMB, SOUTH GATE
Sikrandra / *c* 1612 A.D.
*This example of architecture under
the Mughals where the Islamic forms
met these of Hinduism.*

§ 115 Akbar's Tomb, South Gate
This detail shows the intricacy of the
inlaid stonework.

§ 116 AKBAR'S TOMB
Sikrandra / *c* 1612 A.D.

§ 117 ITIMAD-UD-DAULA'S TOMB
Agra / *c* 1628 A.D.
*The decor of pietra dura inlay
and marble mosaic create a
surface elegant in its simplicity.*

§ 118 & § 119 Taj Mahal
Agra / White marble / 1628–56 A.D.
The justly famous tomb of Mumtaj sits in calm splendor in the panoramic view above while maintaining its beauty as the onlooker comes closer (below) to examine its inlay work.

§ 120 SCREEN
Taj Mahal, Agra / White marble / 1628–1656 A.D.
The perforated screens with lapidary work and
pietra-dura inlay on the cenotaph relieve the
cold air of the tomb and add a lyrical grace.

§ 121 SHRINE AT TIRUVANNAMALAJ
Tiruvannamalaj / 17th c. A.D.
*Typical of the final development of
Hindu temples in South India is this
giant, enclosed temple precinct.
The four gates are larger than the
smaller central shrine.*

§ 122 & § 123 MINAKSHI TEMPLE AT MADURA
Madura / Masonry and stucco / 17th c. A.D.
*At right and also in background at left is one of
the great gates (gopuran) of a temple complex.
Built up of ascending planes, the structure's
unity and continuity are threatened by the mul-
titudinous images and intricate ornamentation.
The tank, left, is used for ritual ablution and
is an innovation of South Indian architecture.*

§ 124 GOPIS IN ARBOR (ABOVE)
Nayagarh / Painting on paper / late 17th c. A.D.
Asutosh Museum, Calcutta
Milkmaids (gopis) *await Krishna in this masterpriece of
Orissa tradition. Agitated lines add to the emotional
aspects of their waiting.*

§ 125 POLO (BELOW)
Mughal court / Painting on paper / 30 × 20 cm
18th c. A.D. / National Museum, New Delhi
*Late example of court painting in which the miniaturist
brings out the quick movements of the emperor's favorite
game against a carefully composed landscape background.*

§ 126 ANIMAL FABLE
Mughal school / Painting on paper / *c* 1595 A.D.
Bharat Kala Bhavan, Banaras
A royal copy with twenty-seven illustrations of
the Akbar school depicting animal fables, this
work is typical of a type popular in the Islamic
court of the Mughals. Its composition and naturalism
contrast to Indian-inspired works of Rajput.

§ 127 WATER SPORTS OF KRISHNA AND THE GOPIS
Kangra / Painting on paper / 30 × 22 *cm* / 1780–1800 A.D.
Bharat Kala Bhavan, Banaras
The two scenes depicted on this page are typical of
many miniatures which depict Krishna engaged in divine
play with the gopis *(milkmaids). The stories come*
from the Indian epics (this one is from the Bhagavata)
and the adventures of the god Krishna are a popular subject.
Krishna is generally depicted in a blue shade.

§ 128 KRISHNA STEALING THE GOPIS' CLOTHES
Kangra / Painting on paper / 21.5 × 15 *cm*
late 18th c. A.D. / Bharat Kala Bhavan, Banaras
(detail reproduced in color on the jacket)

§ 129 FEMALE ATTENDANTS
Kangra / Painting on paper / 18th c. A.D.
Villiers David Coll., London

§ 130 Lady Smoking a Hukka
Decani / Painting on paper / 1725–50 A.D.
Bharat Kala Bhavan, Benaras
*Highly decorative and very Indian in its way
of depicting the faces and costumes of the lady
and her attendant in this miniature.*

§ 131 RADHA AND KRISHNA
Kangra / Painting on paper / 18th c. A.D.
Lucknow Museum, Uttar Pradesh
The theme is Hindu but the treatment is Mughal.
The Pahari school included many local schools.
Here, refugee painters from the plains who settled
in the Himalayan region dwelt on various aspects
of emotion mainly through the Radha-Krishna love
theme so popular in Hindu miniatures.

§ 132 Mandapa Ceiling Painting (LEFT)
Devi Shrine, Nataraja Temple,
Chidambaram
c 17th c. A.D.
*This work, on the north side of the inner bay,
depicts the story of Darukavanam.*

§ 133 Krishnalila
Midnapore / Scroll painting on paper
52.5 × 75 *cm* / 19th c. A.D.
Author's Coll.
*The Patuas (folk painters) of Bengal deal with
a wide range of themes, including popular
mythology (here, about krishna). They appeal
directly to the eye, without subterfuge,
avoiding the vague fantasy which had been
evolved in Indian iconography and which
led to the betrayal of fundamental form.
Moreover, these Pata paintings are collective
creations, the teamwork of several family
members.*

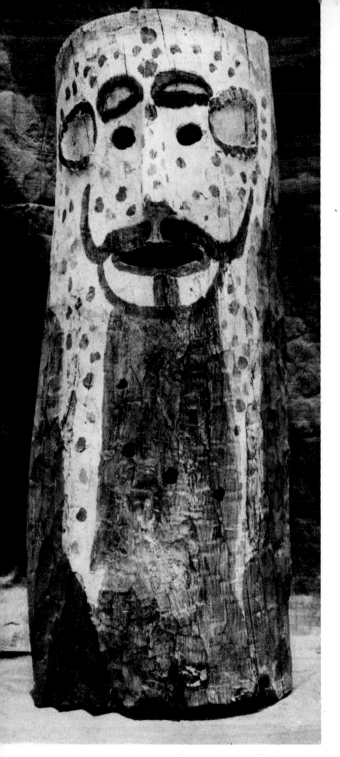

§ 134 Scarecrow
Chhindwara, Madhya Pradesh / Painted wood
20th c. A.D. / Indian Tribal Research Coll.
*This object is intended for the use the title
indicates—not as an ornament. It is carved
out of a block of wood with a hole made to
house a pole so that the scarecrow may be set
up in a field to frighten away animals and birds.*

§ 135 Man Thinking
Wood / 20th c. A.D.
National Museum, New Delhi
*Tribe members like to carve in
wood, here having produced a human
in basic outline, but with an attempt
at naturalization by affixing hair.*

§ 137 BIRTH OF THE BUDDHA
By Nandalal Bose / Tempera / 20th c. A.D.
G.D. Birla Coll., Calcutta

Nandalal, the foremost disciple of Abanindranath, has been much influenced by Indian classical art, especially that of Ajanta. Though small, the work has the qualities of a mural.

§ 136 MOTHER AND CHILD
Parganas / Painted clay / 10.2 *cm* high
24 Pargans Asutosh Museum, Calcutta

This folk doll, painted in yellow and vermilion mixed with milk, is a remarkable variation on the mother and child theme. The simplicity is reminiscent of modern sculpture.

Tribal & Modern Art 149

§ 138 Head
By Jamini Roy / Tempera / 20th c. A.D.
Author's Coll.
In his exploration in the field of forms, Jamini
Roy breaks new ground. A work of the earlier phase
of his quest, bold in color and simple in execution.

§ 140 (UNTITLED)
By Rabindranath Tagore / Watercolor
20th c. A.D. / Rabindra-Sadana,
Santiniketan

§ 139 MOTHER and CHILD
Rabindranath Tagore / Watercolor
20th c. A.D. / Rabindra-Sadana,
Santiniketan

§ 141 CATS
By Jamini Roy / Tempera on cardboard
71 × 56 cm / Thomas J. Needham Coll., U.S.A.

Prehistoric Periods: Hand-axes, scrapers, flints, knives, etc., from Kashmir, Mayurbhanj, Guntur, Nellore, Guddapah, Kurnool and some parts of Madhya pradesh. NEOLITHIC: Celts, ring-stones, hammer-stones from Chotanagpur, Orissa, Bengal, and Assam. Cave paintings of Madhya Pradesh and Uttar Pradesh, notably at Singapur, Hoshangabad and Mirzapur. MEGALITHIC: Dolmens, menhirs, cromlechs, burial jars and mounds in Sind, South and Western India. Dravidian civilization.

Indus Valley Culture c. 3000-1500 B.C.: Steatite seals and bronze figures, jewellery, painted pottery, terracotta figurines from Harappa, Mohenjo-daro, Chanhu-daro, etc.

Aryan Settlement (Vedic Period) c. 1500-800 B.C.: Rig Veda, c. 800 B. C. Earth Goddess and Vedic burial mounds, etc. from Lauriya-Nandangarh and Bhita. 800 B. C. Upanishads.

Saisunga Dynasty c. 642-322 B.C.: Mahavira 599–527 B. C., Buddha 563–483 B. C. Jataka stories 500–200 B. C.

Maurya Dynasty 322-185 B.C.: Yaksha figures, black pottery, terracotta figurines from Patna, Basarh, Set-Mahet, etc. 272-232 B.C. Asoka: Monolithic pillars, rock-edicts, early cave architecture.

Sunga & Kanva Dynasties 185-28 B.C.: Sculptured gateways and railings of Bharhut, Sanchi and Bodhgaya.

Parthian & Saka Dynasties c. 60 B.C.-48A.D.: Early Gandhara sculptures.

Kushan Dynasties c. 30-250 A.D.: Continuing traditions of sculpture in Gandhara and Mathura. Origin of Buddha image. Around 67 A. D. Buddhism reaches China.

Andhra Dynasties 230 B.C.-225 A.D.: Sculptured stupas at Amaravati and Nagarjuni-kunda. Clay figures from Kundapur.

Gupta Dynasty 320-600 A.D.: Golden Age of Indian art and literature. Main centres of sculpture Mathura and Sarnath. Stone and brick temples at Deogarh, Bhitargaon, etc. Murals at Ajanta and Bagh, contemporary murals at Sigiriya, Ceylon; Bamiyan Afganistan; and Tun Huang, Central Asia.

Early Medievel Dynasties 7th-10th c. A.D.: Pallava Dynasty, c. 325–700 A. D. Rock-out shrines and sculptures at Mahabalipuram. Chalukya Dynasty, 550-642 A. D. The Descent of the Ganges Temples at Badami and Aihole. Rashtrakuta Dynasty, 757-973 A. D. Kailasa temple and murals at Elura; cave temple at Elephanta. Pala Dynasty, c. 750–1100 A. D. Stone and metal sculptures and illustrated manuscripts. Sculptors: Dhiman and Bitpalo.

Indian Art Abroad 8th-10th c. A.D.: Borobudur and Prambanam in Java. Angkor Wat and Angkor Thom in Cambodia. Hindu rule in East Java, 10th to 16th century A. D. Temples at Pagan in Burma. Thousand Buddhas in Lung-men caves in China. Horyuji temple at Nara in Japan.

Late Medieval Dynasties 11th-15th c. AD.: Temples at Khajuraho. Solankis of Gujarat, 765–1197 A. D. Jain temples at Mount Abu, Girnar, etc. Eastern Gangas of Orissa, 1076–1148 A. D. Temples at Bhuvanesvar, Konarak, and Puri. Chola Dynasty, 907–1053 A. D. Temples at Tanjore, South Indian bronzes, images of Nataraja. Hoysala and Yadava Dynasties, 1111–1318 A.D. Temples at Halebid and Belur.

Sultanate of Delhi 1206-1586 A.D.: Early Indo-Islamic architecture.

Mughal Empire 1526-1802 A.D.: Mughal architecture at Delhi, Agra, Fatehour Sikri, Allahabad, etc. Mughal gardens at Lahore and Srinagar. Mughal paintings 17th to 19th century A. D. Rajput and Pahari paintings.

Colonial and Modern Periods 18th-20th c. A.D.: Archaeological Survey of India. Folk arts and crafts and primitive survivals. Benghal School, Abanindranath Tagore, Nandalal Bose, Jamini Roy.

The Arts of India: CHRONOLOGY

18 Weeping woman

23-24 Bud life (Bigi Tree)

37 Gandba

75 Hands #51   #21
79 Bracet   96
87-88 lovers #54
105 Celestial dan   Bracket figure #55
114-5 Abstan tut
124-5
137

THE CHRONOLOGY IS ON THE OPPOSITE SIDE OF
THIS FOLD-OUT FLAP. THIS FEATURE ALLOWS
THE READER TO CONSULT THE CHRONOLOGY
AT THE SAME TIME HE IS LOOKING AT THE
PLATES OR THE TEXT.